Write a Book in a Weekend: 7 "Insider" Strategies

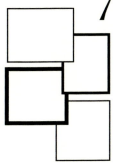

Find the Time, Choose a Winning Topic & Get Your Book Done!
For Coaches, Consultants, Service Professionals & Entrepreneurs

Donna Kozik
Creator & Leader: "Write a Book in a Weekend" Events

Copyright © 2009 Donna Kozik.

All rights reserved. No portion of this book may be reproduced mechanically, electronically, or by any other means, including photocopying, without written permission of the publisher. It is illegal to copy this book, post it to a website, or distribute it by any other means without permission from the publisher.

Donna Kozik
San Diego, Calif.
Phone: 619-297-1749

Email: Donna@MyBigBusinessCard.com

Websites: www.WriteWithDonna.com
www.MyBigBusinessCard.com

Social Media: www.Facebook.com/DonnaKozik
www.Twitter.com/DonnaKozik
Connect with me on "Linked In"

Limits of Liability and Disclaimer of Warranty
The author and publisher shall not be liable for your misuse of this material. This book is strictly informational and educational purposes.

Warning – Disclaimer
The purpose of this book is to educate and entertain. The author and/or publisher do not guarantee that anyone following these techniques, suggestions, tips, ideas, or strategies will become successful. The author and/or publisher shall have neither liability nor responsibility to anyone with respect to any loss or damage caused, or alleged to be caused, directly or indirectly by the information contained in this book.

ISBN: 978-0-9740019-6-8

Pictured on Cover
"Write a Book in a Weekend" Graduates

Sheila B
Think, Act and Succeed! An Inspirational Success Guide to Tickle Your Imagination and Trigger Action!

Rosie Battista
52 Ways to Fall in Love with Your Food, with Your Body, with Your Life

Pamela Bruner
Make Your Success Easy

Tom Buford
Charge What You Deserve: The Lifestyle Fee-Setting Formula Revealed: What Every Service Professional Should Know Before Charging Their Next Client

Jeff Cadwell
After the Diagnosis: The Journey Beyond

Renia Carsillo
One Man, One Show: 21 Seeks to Profitable Self-Employment

Kelli Corasanti
Kelli's Quips: Happy Thoughts for Busy People

Susan Daffron
Funds to the Rescue: 101 Fundraising Ideas for Humane and Animal Rescue Groups

Vicki Ehlers
Green at Birth: Smart Mothers Create Nature Connections for Infants & Toddlers

Sandy Goodwin
I Think, Therefore I Doubt: 12 Key Principles to Build Self-Confidence & Self-Trust for Perfectionists, People-Pleasers, and Heart-Centered Women

Peggy Lee Hanson
Fiftysomething: The Unknown, Dreams and Paths

Laymon Hicks
Unleash the Passion for Your Purpose and *A Treasure Chest of Motivation*

Maggie Keenan
Small Businesses Give Big

Meredith Liepelt
Flourish! 10 Easy, Elegant and Essential Marketing Strategies for Solo- and Micropreneurs

Carma Spence-Potthit
Home Sweet Home Page: 5 Deadly Mistakes Authors, Speakers and Coaches Make with Their Website's Home Page & How to Fix Them!

Peter Wallin
In Pursuit of Business: Sell More, Grow More, Earn More…Live More

Rev. Karen Weingard
I Am the Party: Set for Life and Lovin' It

Ron J. West
The Perfect Life: A Personal Journey of Relationship Healing

Acknowledgements & Dedication

My heartfelt appreciation to the following people for being big believers in MyBigBusinessCard.com and my dream:

    Sister and brother-in-law, Teresa and Brad Castleman
    Super Best Friend, Marjorie Old
    Best bud and "29 Days" co-author, Tara Maras
    More-than-just-a-staff-member, Michelle Dimsey
    "My big business card" idea generator, client and friend, Peter Wallin

And, especially, Adam Urbanski, for saying the magical words, "You should start a group on Facebook. Call it the 'Write a Book in a Weekend Club.'"

Finally, my "eggs-traordinary" business manager and Number One, Dina Rocha. Thank you for hounding me to get this and so much more done—and laughing with me all the way.

■ ■ ■

This book is dedicated to all my past, present and future authors. I am so, so proud of you!

> "You are never given a wish without also being given the power to make it come true."
>
> ~ Richard Bach

What Others Say About Donna Kozik & Her "Write a Book in a Weekend" Virtual Event

"You Make It Do-able and Simple"

"I'm a hard guy to please. I'm very demanding. I'm the harshest judge of my own programs. I am merciless when I evaluate other people's programs. And I'm not kidding—I was really impressed in what you put together.

"I liked the fact that you inspired and motivated me. Your program was just fantastic and provided that motivation and spark to just get going. The structure, the calls, the emails, the printed guide…I loved it.

"If there was one thing that I was so amazed and in awe of that I think is worth mentioning above all else, is that you make it so **doable and so simple**.

"I can't stop talking about it. Donna, I really think you did a brilliant job!" '

Adam Urbanski
TheMarketingMentors.com
Irvine, Calif.

"I Now Have My Book In Hand"

"I followed Donna's program exactly as she presented and now have my book in hand—I couldn't have done it without her or the 'Write a Book in a Weekend' online event.

"She made it so easy and simple—I love how she laid everything out step-by-step and was available throughout the weekend to answer my questions and guide me through the process. She's a natural leader—and made writing my book fun!"

Vicki Ehlers,
Stillwater, Okla.
Author, *Green at Birth: Smart Moms Create Nature Connections for Infants & Toddlers*
GreenAtBirth.com

"One of the Greatest Things Is How Easy It Can Be"

"I was blown away…one of the greatest things Donna offers is **how easy it can be.** When we think about books we think about it being an arduous process, Donna broke it down in clear steps. She's passionate and compassionate about showing us how we could do it in a weekend, and then take the product from the weekend to **use as a platform** for ourselves and a stepping stone to new opportunities."

Suzanne Evans
HelpMorePeople.com

"Anything Related to Books, Donna Is the Person to Talk To!"

"Donna is beyond amazing. She has really helped me take my book from dream to reality.

"I believe if you really want to learn this business with book marketing—or anything related to books—she is the person to talk to. She is there to help you, to guide you and to really be a resource. Use her services and, more importantly, become a friend because she's there to help."

Laymon Hicks
LaymonHicks.com
Author, "Treasure Chest of Motivation" & "Unleash the Passion for Your Purpose"

"I Really Don't Consider Myself a Writer…This Opened My Eyes"

"The biggest takeaway I got from 'Write a Book in a Weekend' is to expand my thinking about what a book is. I thought it had to be 300 pages, wall-to-wall writing, and from the discussions I realized there are a lot of different book sizes, some as little as 64 pages, that have value.

"I really don't consider myself a writer and this opened my eyes to me thinking this is possible. I really enjoyed it and I definitely recommend this to other business people."

Linda Griffin
Ashburn, Va.
CareerShock.com

Contents

Who Is Donna Kozik?	15
Is This Book for You?	21

The First Four Insider Strategies:
Fast & Easy Ideas from the "Write a Book in a Weekend" Coach
25

# 1. Get Cooking on Your Book & Recite Your Favorite Recipe	27
# 2. Write Your Book Like You Would Clean Your Closet	31
# 3. Visualize Your Book & Download It into Reality	35
# 4. Should You Self-Publish or Traditional Publish?	39

The Final Three Insider Strategies:
Write a Short & Powerful Book
43

(Mini Book Examples)

# 5. The Quote Book	47
# 6. The 'Ezine Article/Blog Posting' Book	71
# 7. The Case Study Book	85
Bringing It All Together	95
Words of Appreciation & Resources	101

Who Is Donna Kozik?

Donna Kozik grew up on a 200-acre dairy farm in northwestern Pennsylvania and now lives near the freeways and beaches of San Diego, where she shows coaches, entrepreneurs and others how to become published authors the "fast and easy way."

In fact, she has set a personal goal of turning 1000 people into published authors in the next 12 months.

Her system for doing this is virtual "Write a Book in a Weekend" events, featuring Donna's "fill-in-the-blanks" book template plus a weekend of live audio and recorded video messages that motivate and inspire soon-to-be-authors to complete their books in two days.

She is a former newspaper editor and senior communications specialist, a two-time award winning book author. Her first book *29 Days to a Smooth Move: A Household Moving Manual,* co-authored with Tara Maras, led her to be featured in *Woman's Day* and *Women's World* magazines, *The LA Times* and *The Baltimore Sun* newspapers, and NPR's "Marketplace" news magazine. She's also been a paid national media spokesperson for Sprint PCS and has been featured in several other books including ones by Bob Bly and MarketingProfs, along with *Don't Sweat the Small Stuff—and It's All Small Stuff Stories* and *The Vision Board: The Secret to an Extraordinary Life* published by Harper Collins.

To find out more about how you can write a book in a weekend, plus get a free audio "12 Strategies for Publishing Success" and book writing resource guide, visit www.WriteWithDonna.com.

Get Your Free Companion Audio & Resource Guide Here

"Inside Author Tips: 5 Sizzling Strategies to Get Your Book Done on the Double"

Featuring two-time award winning author Donna Kozik (as seen in *Woman's Day* & *Women's World* magazines, plus heard on NPR's "Marketplace")

Listen to this companion audio and discover:

1. The single most important reason why most people never get their book done. (Never fall prey to it again!)
2. 5 simple strategies that will allow you to get your book done in your "spare time".
3. Insider secrets to writing the kind of book that everyone wants to read! Get the scoop on what turns a "blah" book into a "best seller" material.
4. 3 proven methods to "write without writing" for writingphobes and those who fear writer's block!
5. Mindset mastery. How to stop procrastinating and "getting in your own way" when it comes to writing or finishing your book. Donna notes: This might be listed last but I've found that it's the most important item that turns "wannabe" writers into published authors.

You're guaranteed to be inspired and ready to get started writing your own masterpiece or "big business card."

Get your FREE companion audio at
www.MyBigBusinessCard.com/fivestrategies

"Give me the straight scoop. What's this 'Write a Book in a Weekend' all about?"

It's a "virtual" online weekend, when you can create the one item that can lead you to:

- Get more of the highly coveted clients you desire
- Charge higher fees—even as much as quadrupling your current asking price
- Establish your expertise overnight—expertise that you don't have to explain because no one will question you
- Speak volumes about your professional knowledge and credibility—24 hours a day, 7 days a week!

There's a way to achieve those items and much more—including a feeling of self-satisfaction in doing something so many just dream of doing…

Becoming a published author.

In fact, you probably realize that having your book has become as necessary as having a website or a business card—your book is your business card.

A book has become a proven way to attract more engagements, generate back-of-room sales and provide a starting point for other info products.

Other benefits of having a book include:

- Establishing credibility and expertise in your field
- "Speaks" for you 24/7

- Serves as a lead generator and client attraction tool
- Thanks to technology, easier to publish—for only a few dollars—than ever before

The problem is…you still have to write it!

What generally gets in the way of doing that is:

- Finding the time
- Determining what to write about, whether you're narrowing down a broad topic or "starting from scratch"
- Figuring out how to organize your materials
- Banishing your inner critic
- Knowing if you're on the right path

Before I go on, I want to give you a few starter solutions:

1. Write a "short and powerful" book— that is short on content, but still powerful in message (and can be written fast!)

2. Types of short and powerful books you can write include a quote book, a book of case studies, even a book based on questions you receive all the time. (If people are asking, they want to know.)

3. Still stuck? Look to your email "sent" box for material you've already written. Some of the answers you email in response to client questions can practically be taken word for word and put in a book.

This gives you a clearer direction and can make it seem more manageable.

Umm, of course, you STILL have to write it!

That's why I developed the "Write a Book in a Weekend" virtual event. It's a program and a system to literally have you write a book in a weekend. (Plus give you the publishing know-how so you can have a copy in hand the following week!)

I'll tell you in a moment how you can register…plus get a free gift from me.

But first, here are some highlights of my "Write a Book in a Weekend" system:

- Write from the comfort of your own home (no travel necessary)
- Still get the "event" feel with people you can network with
- Book "templates" take care of the formatting for you
- An expert "book writing coach" giving you feedback and answering your questions
- An "after care" program that shows you what to do after the weekend to market yourself and your book
- Bonus audios about selecting a winning title, organizing your material, effectively scheduling your time and much, much more.

To find when the next "Write a Book in a Weekend" Event is, visit www.WriteWithDonna.com. While you're there, register for my free audio, "12 Strategies to Publishing Success," plus pick up your copy of my free publishing resource guide.

Is This Book for You?

> "You are never given a wish without also being given the power to make it come true."
>
> ~Richard Bach, writer

If you are a coach, consultant or entrepreneur you know the benefits of being a published author. A book establishes your expertise, builds your credibility and can be used in a number of ways to generate more warm leads, hot prospects and steady clients. Plus, the additional exposure your book brings you means you can raise your fees and people will pay it—no questions asked!

In fact, you probably realize that having your book has become as necessary as having a website or a business card—in fact, your book *is* your business card.

A book has become a proven way to attract more engagements, generate back-of-room sales and provide a starting point for other info products.

Yet if you've tried to write you book, you know there can be some challenges in getting started—or getting finished…

1. **It's hard and time-consuming work to write a book.**

    You've probably heard the statistic that four out of five of us want to write a book. The fact is, few of us realize that dream. Let's face it, **writing a book is hard work**. It doesn't take just a little bit of time—it can take **a lot of time.** With so many things pulling at our attention, it's hard to find the hours needed to sit down and write.

Perhaps you've even scheduled some "book writing time" in your appointment book and held true to a couple of them, but then found things going by the wayside as other items to take priority.

Or maybe things stalled as you realized that writing a book was a much bigger project than you originally thought, and you became frustrated by the process.

Don't feel bad—I started and stopped my second book several times before finally getting it done. It can be a frustrating process, especially when you're trying to do it on your own with sheer willpower. As a friend of mine says, "Willpower is so '80's!"

2. **You don't know how to select a "winning topic."**

    Say you do have the time and the energy to write a book, how do you know what to write about? Whether you've been working in your field for awhile or are just getting started, you probably have a fairly large "knowledge base." How do you pick one of your own "hot topics" and then narrow or expand the subject matter for a book?

    Next, how do you make sure your book is one people will want to read? Just like you wouldn't stand up and start speaking about anything, your book has to have purpose and focus so it connects to your audience. You'll agree that you don't want to waste your time putting a book together that's not going to speak well of you when you're done, right?

3. **Where do you even begin in organizing your thoughts for "book format?"**

    Sure, you might have put together your fair share of ezine articles and blog posts, and have thought about compiling them into a book—but what comes next? And what else do you have to worry about so your book and its content can stand proudly on the shelf next to other books at Borders and Barnes & Noble?

Most of all, where do you go to get it published? You're a business owner, after all, and don't want to put the time and effort into learning a whole new skill like publishing. There are hundreds of places online claiming they can print and publish your book, but how do you know who to trust?

4. **You really don't consider yourself a writer.**

    Or, maybe you're one who doesn't put together ezine articles or blog posts. Maybe you do most of your work face to face or on the phone and don't have a "back end" of articles and other written material. How can you write a book when you don't have "word one" done? I'm here to tell you that you definitely can—and I show you how.

5. **You've heard that it costs 100s, if not 1000s, of dollars to get a book "done right."**

    You may have been hearing the debate about being self-published versus pursuing a traditional publisher. If you do self-publish there are thousands of companies to consider—how do you know which is the right one?

    I understand—anybody would find all these challenges overwhelming. (I know I did when I published my first book several years ago—years before all these options sprung up all over the place!) I also understand that you're not in the "publishing" business—you have your own area of expertise and little time to figure out the best way to get your book published.

    Even though everyone can have an opinion, the answers to your publishing questions will become crystal clear once you know the pros and cons of each method, and even several scenarios where you can have the best of both worlds!

It was problems like these that led me to develop the online virtual "Write a Book in Weekend" event as the ultimate solution: a fast and easy way to get published and create the ultimate positioning tool to use as a lead generator, expertise builder and have clients pursing you—not the other way around!

I've created a signature system so you can create a book that will generate attention, interest and turn on the tap to a huge gush of leads. And I give you everything you need to do it in one short weekend.

If you'd like to know more, read on!

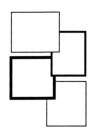 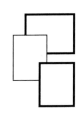

The First Four Insider Strategies:

Fast & Easy Ideas from the "Write a Book in a Weekend" Coach

1. Get Cooking on Your Book & Recite Your Favorite Recipe

2. Write Your Book Like You Would Clean Your Closet

3. Visualize Your Book & Download It into Reality

4. Should You Self-Publish or Traditional Publish?

Insider Strategy
#1

Get Cooking on Your Book & Recite Your Favorite Recipe

> "My recipe for life is not being
> afraid of myself, afraid of what I think
> or of my opinions."
>
> ~ Eartha Kitt

Many times when people struggle about what to write about I bring up…food! Leave the book writing realm for a moment and think about one of your favorite recipes. The dish you take places and have people clustering around you asking how you made it. Now think about your description of that recipe and all the steps involved.

For example, take a lasagna recipe. Most of them are the same—layers of meat, cheese and noodles. But I have a "super lasagna" recipe—one that when I took it places, it wasn't long before I was cornered with demands of "how do you make it?"

I usually start describing my cheese layer, which is a combination of four cheeses: ricotta, parmesan, cottage and mozzarella. (Hey, I didn't say it was a low-calorie lasagna!) I also add garlic salt and parsley—a little more of this, a little pinch of that. You can see how a seemingly simple recipe gets more complex. Mix it all together, metaphorically speaking—and you have a lasagna recipe that was mine and mine alone. I had taken a basic one and added my own special touches.

I've made it so often, it's no problem for me to describe it to my friends, who write fast to get every ingredient and its amount down. But here's the key: Because I've made it dozens of times, it's easy for me to make it and easy for me to describe. Others interested in making it ask questions and make sure they get the ingredients, order of preparation and over temperature down right. But it's simple…TO ME.

Now back to you and your book. There's a "favorite recipe," or something you know how to do in your business, for instance, that's seemingly simple on the outside, but complex once you delve into it. And it's something that other people want to know how to do—it solves a problem for them.

And the good news, no the absolutely great, fantastic, super duper news, is that you can base an entire book on this recipe.

Action step: Identify your "killer recipe" and think about the steps (soon to be chapters) involved in its creation.

Insider Strategy
#2

Write Your Book Like You Would Clean Your Closet

> "I like my money
> right where I can see it...
> hanging in my closet."
>
> ~ Sarah Jessica Parker

Many aspiring authors get overwhelmed with material. They are overwhelmed with so much research and items to include in their book, they don't know where to start.

Well, it's time to go to the closet!

If you're like me, there are times where you closet is crammed to full to bursting forth with clothes of all kinds—fall, winter, spring, summer in a one place.

So you decide to clean it, starting with taking everything out and draping it over the bed, dresser, chairs and, as a last resort, the floor. You're feeling better because the closet is empty—you're starting with a clean slate, but turn around and you're overwhelmed all over again.

One effective method I use for putting items back in that closet is first choosing the outfits I know I look good in and serve as the basis of my wardrobe…the sexy outfit for date night, the power outfit for presentations, the comfy outfit for rainy days. Those are my "basics" that I know for sure will go back in my closet. And, again, if you're like me, there are five or so of these outfits.

The rest of the items might go in there, they might go to Goodwill. But once I have my staples—the ones I know I look good in—I'm feeling much better about things.

So, when writing your book and overwhelmed with material, here's what I suggest you do:

1. Briefly revisit your research and notes. The key is to *move quickly* through them and not get bogged down in re-reading everything. (When I'm cleaning out my closet, I don't try on every item I take out. It's like that.)

2. Highlight or put a sticky by the items you deem important—they have a good chance of making it into your book.

3. Put all your notes away. Close the documents on screen and file away the hard copy notes until they are out of site.

4. Open a new document or get out a clean sheet of paper.

5. Write down the gist of "5 things you know for sure." The big picture items that will make up the core messages of your book.

You have just created what I call your "Power Outline." This clean and neat document will serve as the foundation of your book.

Insider Strategy
#3

Visualize Your Book & Download It into Reality

> "People only see
> what they are prepared to see."
>
> ~ Ralph Waldo Emerson

Still having trouble visualizing *your* book? Yes, sometimes the idea can remain nebulous until you start putting your own together. Plus, the idea of writing can still seem a little bit scary and like work.

So let's take a "fun break" and put creativity to work, while making it more "real" in your eyes. (This is another recommendation I make to my "Write a Book in a Weekend" participants when they join the virtual weekend event.)

1. Find a book that's similar in size and page count to yours; one that has a format and layout you would like too. Keep it nearby to refer to and also serve as inspiration as you see your book taking shape.

2. Create a "prototype" of your book. Take a three ring binder and, in 30 minutes or so (Read: don't make it a big project), create a mock front and back cover of your book.

3. Elements to include on the front cover:
    a. Your title and subtitle
    b. Testimonial from a leader in your field
    c. Picture of yourself

4. Elements to include on the back cover:
    a. Attention getting headline
    b. Bullet points of what people will find inside

    c. More testimonials

    d. Price, category, ISBN number and UPC code

The more complete and "official" looking the better! As your book starts taking shape, you can print out and put pages in your book, including title page, dedication, acknowledgements, contents, and, of course, your drafted and completed chapters.

The beauty of this exercise is that it works really well for those of us who want to really see things taking shape. It's like creating your vision before your very eyes. Plus, you can carry it around to work on when you have a spare moment, Finally, it will impress people when you show it to them, and they will keep you accountable by asking "when will your book be published?"

Insider Strategy #4

Should You Self-Publish of Traditional Publish?

The First Four Insider Strategies

*"If we would have new knowledge,
we must get a whole world of new questions."*

~ Susanne K. Langer

The question of how to publish your book is grappled with by aspiring authors everywhere. On the heels of the above question come several more:

- Will self-publishing hurt my chances of being published by a traditional publisher?
- How hard is it to be picked up by a traditional publisher?
- How long will I have to wait before I can hold my book in my hands?
- If I do self-publish, where should I go?

First, let's go over some definitions.

Self publishing means YOU are the publisher of record and oversee all the editing, printing, publicity, and distribution arrangements of your book, plus assume all the financial risk of your book project. (It also means you control it from beginning to end.)

Traditional publishing means a company, usually one that is in the business of publishing many authors, edits, prints and distributes your book. Sometimes it helps with promotion, but more and more often it doesn't (at least not to a great extent).

Two important characteristics of both traditional and self-publishing:

1. Both use the same printing presses, meaning both can produce the same physical quality of book.
2. Because they carry more of the risk, the *publisher* of the book most often makes the most money from the book.

Ideally, an author is published both ways—traditional and self, which means greater distribution and money making options.

It used to be traditional publishers shied away of taking on a book that was originally self-published. Thankfully, times have changed. In fact, traditional publishers have done a "180" and welcome self-published works because of two items the author can bring:

1. A clear message.
2. A platform for that message.

Platform refers to a built in audience for the author's message and authors who bring a proven message and an audience saying they want to read it will move to the front of the line in any publisher's office.

Still doubtful? Have you heard of these books?

What Color Is Your Parachute? by Richard N. Bolles. This guide for job seekers, has been on the *New York Times* best-seller list periodically for more than a decade and was originally self-published/

The One Minute Manager by Kenneth Blanchard and Spencer Johnson, was self-published before the authors sold it to William Morrow & Company. It was one of the biggest-selling hardcover books of the 1980s.

Rich Dad, Poor Dad was written by Robert Kiyosaki, with Sharon Lechter, in 1997 as a $15.95 "brochure" designed to attract customers to a website where Kiyowsaki could sell a $195 board game. After selling rights to Warner Business Books in 2000 and appearing on *Oprah*, he sold millions more copies, with the book sitting on the *New York Times* bestseller list for four years.

(Sources: New York Times and John Kremer)

I also heard Jack Canfield say he and Mark Victor Hansen would have self-published *Chicken Soup for the Soul* if it hadn't been picked up by a traditional publisher. Jack went on to say there is nothing wrong with self-publishing.

No matter how you do it, there's power and prestige in being a published author. Period.

The Final Three Insider Strategies:

Write a Short & Powerful Book

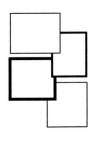
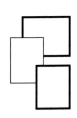

Mini Book Examples:

\# 5.   The Quote Book

\# 6.   The 'Ezine Article/Blog Posting' Book

\# 7.   The Case Study Book

Write a Short & Powerful Book

One of the keys to success for my "Write a Book in a Weekend" participants is what I call the "short and powerful" book. This is a book that's short on words, but powerful in message. It's a true example of quality versus quantity. The beauty of the short and powerful book is that it *still is a viable book*. In other words, it still establishes your credibility and expertise, and makes you a true published author, but it does it without causing you to have to write *War and Peace*.

In this section I give three examples of "short and powerful" books you can write in a weekend.

- The Quote Book
    - Quote Book Example 1: Just the Quotes
    - Quote book Example 2: Quotes Plus Commentary
- The Ezine Article/Blog Posting Book
- The Case Study Book

After that I bring it all together and then describe ways you can get started on your book today!

Insider Strategy
#5

The Quote Book

Everyone loves quotes—those words of wisdom spoken by the leaders who came before us and the leaders of our time. If you're like me, they are on your desk, your refrigerator, your bathroom mirror—anywhere whre you need an extra push of encouragement or inspiration.

Did you know that you can take your favorite quotes and make a book out of them? You can! Quote books are not only easy to create, they are also the types of books that are actually read. In addition, those readers keep these books near by for instant inspiration and motivation. (Perfect if you're a coach, fitness pro or anyone looking to lead and inspire others.)

Here are the basic steps for creating a quote book:

1. Collect and organize according to theme a large number of quotes. I recommend anywhere between 60 and 200. Also sprinkle in a fair amount of "quotable quotes" from yourself, the author. That will instantly elevate your status, too, even if you're quoting yourself in your own book.

2. Put a quote on each page.

3. You can call yourself "done" at this point, if you like, leaving your book's introduction, about the author, front matter and back matter to speak to your expertise and serve as a call to action. Or you can take it a step further and…

4. Add a few paragraphs under each quote. The first can be three to five sentences describing why you selected the quote and what it means to you—in other words, what greater insight it provides beyond the words. The last paragraph on the page can be a "take action" step for your reader to apply the information and inspiration to their own life.

5. Put together 60 or more pages of quotes and you have yourself a great little book to use as a "big business card" people will refer to time after time.

In this section I provide two ways you could do a quote book—the "Just the Quotes" method and the "Quotes Plus Commentary" Method, plus give you some more book writing inspiration along the way.

Just the Quotes

With a "Just the Quotes" style book, you'll provide a go-to resource of inspiration for your readers. If you choose to do this type of book, I recommend making your book's "about the author" and introduction especially strong, and also include front matter and back matter, so your book is a true "big business card."

COURAGE

Looking for words of wisdom to inspire courage in yourself and your writing? These quotes were selected just for you.

> "A ship in port is safe,
> but that's not what ships are built for."
>
> ~ Grace Hopper,
> American Computer Scientist

"If you have a talent, use it in every which way possible. Don't hoard it. Don't dole it out like a miser. Spend it lavishly like a millionaire intent on going broke."

~ Brendan Francis

> "Don't be afraid to take
> a big step if needed.
> You can't cross a chasm in two small jumps."
>
> ~ Anonymous

> "Don't bother just to be better than your contemporaries or predecessors. Try to be better than yourself."
>
> ~ William Faulkner

"You can have anything you want—if you want
it badly enough.
You can be anything you want to be,
have anything you desire, accomplish
anything you set out to accomplish—if you
will hold to that desire
with singleness of purpose."

~Robert Collier

> "Nothing contributes so much to tranquilizing the mind as a steady purpose—a point on which the soul may fix its intellectual eye."
>
> ~ Mary Wollstonecraft Shelley

> "All things are difficult before they are easy."
>
> ~ John Norley

> "Most of our obstacles would melt away if, instead of cowering before them, we make up our minds to walk boldly through them!"
>
> ~ Orison Marden

"All I ask is this: Do something. Try something. Speaking out, showing up, writing a letter, a check, a strongly worded e-mail. Pick a cause—there are few unworthy ones. And nudge yourself past the brink of tacit support to action. Once a month, once a year, or just once."

~ Joss Whedon

> *"Commitment with accountability closes the gap between intention and results."*
>
> ~ Sandra Gallagher

"It's this simple: If you think something will be hard, it will be hard. If you think it will be easy, it will be easy."

~ Donna Kozik
(Yes, you can quote yourself, too!)

Quote Book Example II:
Quotes Plus Commentary

To make your quote book even stronger, include a "mini headline," your thoughts about how you interpret the quote and then give an action step.

> *"I can't change the direction of the wind, but I can adjust my sails to always reach my destination."*
>
> ~ Jimmy Dean

Determine Where You're Going—and Why

When working with my "Write a Book in a Weekend" participants, the first thing I have them do is write a "goal statement" describing why they want to write a book. This serves several purposes. First, there's power in putting it in writing. Second, it helps you develop a crystal clear vision and mission. Finally, it serves as a touchstone if the going gets rough to remind you why you want to be a published author in the first place.

Action step: Write your "goal statement" of why you want to be a published author and how you see your book furthering your life's goals.

> *"Too many people overvalue*
> *what they are not and undervalue*
> *what they are."*
> ~ Malcolm Forbes, Publisher

Recognize Your Greatness

If you're like many aspiring authors, when you think about writing a book you wonder, or maybe even worry, about how it will be different from other books—with the bottom line question being "who will want to read what I have to say?"

But what if you looked at it a different way? Choose to study your book idea from the angle "it may have been said before, but it hasn't been said *my* way!" Your perspective, your wording, your timing in saying what you need to say—all play a role in what will make your book readable.

Write your book—start delivering your message to the world!

Action step: What do you have to say that's *your* unique way of saying it?

"Done is better than perfect."
~ Donna Kozik

'A' Book Doesn't Have to Be 'The' Book

The idea of writing a book can be intimidating because you think it of it not as "A" book but as "THE" book. And that can be getting in the way of getting ANY book done!

Your book doesn't have to be big—it doesn't even have to be perfect (whew!). Instead, it just has to be DONE. And one of the best ways to get it done is to write what I call a "short and powerful" book. One that is short on words, but powerful in message.

Action step: What one "short and powerful" message do you have to share?

> *"Make visible what, without you,*
> *might perhaps never have been seen."*
> ~ Robert Bresson

Share Your Message

This speaks so eloquently to a message I give budding authors all the time. You have a message that is unique—and one that you want to express. You are doing a beautiful thing not only for yourself, but those who will come to read and know your thoughts. Tell your story—share your message—in a book.

What message is uniquely "yours" to share? (Even an acorn of an idea is a start—with time and energy, it will grow into an oak tree!)

Action Step: Are you willing to "stretch your horizons" and go forth to see what is over the next hill? Describe that feeling.

> *"You need to overcome the tug of people against you as you reach for high goals."*
>
> ~ George Patton

Many aspiring authors hold back in getting started because they fear criticism that may come when they're done. When you think about it, it doesn't make much sense to worry about something so far in the future. (And, fact is, sometimes you'll welcome ANY kind of feedback versus no feedback at all.)

But, for now, you can nurture your dream of authoring a book. It's an intimate relationship that starts just between you and the paper or you and the screen. And, if you want, that's as far as it has to go. Ever.

Action Step: What if you pulled back until it was just you and your writing? What would you say?

Insider Strategy #6

The 'Ezine Article/Blog Posting' Book

My favorite writing teacher told me that the secret to his prolific writing was that he "plagiarized himself."

What he meant is that he took items that he already wrote and built upon them for another piece or addressed the same subject from a different angle. Whether you call it multi-purposing, recycling or self-plagiarism, it's an effective way to write your book on the double. Another benefit is that you're building on established messages you've already created. Although many business owners struggle with writing about something new in their ezines and newsletters, the fact is you want to keep to certain themes and points directly related to the products and services you provide.

My formula for writing an "ezine article/blog posting" book:

1. Review the articles you have written to date. Important note: the key here is to move quickly through your pieces. Don't get bogged down by re-reading them word for word—just skim and scan enough to recognize whether or not the piece should go in your book.

2. Put the articles you select in one document on screen. (Think of it as a type of article "parking lot.")

3. Group the articles according to theme.

4. Closely read through and edit for context. Change items that are out of date. Also add additional information where needed.

Following are articles I gathered from my online newsletter and blog to show you how it can be done.

■ ■ ■

How to 'Get Out of Your Own Way'

I've talked to hundreds of people who have been able to get their book started or finished. When I ask them to tell me more, many respond, "I can't get out of my own way." I know what they mean—it seems so easy when you're coaching someone else!

Actually, when you look for things stopping you from being published, it seems there are reasons galore. Frankly, none of these reasons are new or unique to you—they're all the same reasons millions of other authors have faced and managed to overcome.

Here I take on five of the most frequently cited reasons, people give for not getting their book done…in no particular order.

Lack of time. Fact is, we all have the same amount of time—it's up to us about how we choose to use it. And that's done by determining what's important to us and making a commitment. In addition, you might think that writing a book will take longer than it actually does. Alan Cohen has said that if you write three pages a day, in a year you'll have three books! So, if you do the math, you can have one book done in a matter of months. Or, if you compact things a little bit and write a "short and powerful" book like I suggest, you can get it done in a few hours over a weekend.

Lack of subject knowledge. Worried you don't know enough about your subject to write a book about it? Don't be—I'm not kidding when I say you'd be shocked about how much you know. By studying, even for just a little while, whatever subject you're interested in, you know more than most. For some reason, the more we delve into our subject, the more we discount how much we ourselves know. So, trust me, you know your stuff—now just go tell the world!

Lack of writing skill. Not having a lot of experience in formal writing can actually be a positive. Say you're a whiz at writing term papers. Well, who wants to read a book that's written like a term paper? The best books are in a more conversational style, and if you think you're pretty good at writing emails, then you have most likely developed a knack for writing in conversational, yet professional, style.

Lack of "how to do it." Okay, so you get that you can write a book, but then you find yourself hung up on how to get it published. Again, it's pretty easy these days with print-on-demand technology and what's being called "hybrid publishing," which combines the best of both worlds in self-publishing and traditional publishing. I have resources that can tell you more, however first thing's first, and that's getting the book written.

It's funny about what can hold so many of us back from going after our pursuits. Yet there are also many, many books out there—so somebody has to be writing them. Think about your challenges and think of ways to "walk boldly through them!" I've got to tell you, there's nothing like being a published author, and I want you to feel the same feeling I have and others have. Don't get in your own way—get started!

■ ■ ■

Are You REALLY Ready to Become a Published Author?

When you think about everything you've accomplished in this life and in your business, well, I hope you're impressed.

And, if you're not, know that I am impressed by you.

I may not know you personally, however I have complete confidence in saying you put a lot of energy into your life, you are dedicated to your clients and customers and you are an expert at what you do.

And I know all that stemmed from you making a decision. Somewhere along the line you made one decision after another and the result is your current success.

So, if you're now teetering on the decision of whether or not to make now the time to write your book, here are some questions to consider and propel you in one direction or the other.

By the way, even though it's my business to show you how to be a published author sooner rather than later, know that I'm truly not pushing you one way or the other. I know the power of making your own decision—and the ineffectiveness of having that decision made for you. For instance, have you ever had a spouse, parent or other well meaning individual sign you up for a gym membership? Not very inspirational, is it? And I'm guessing it didn't get you to that gym on a regular basis.

Some of us are simply too busy taking care of many clients or have lead generation systems in place that are already working quite well. Others have no need to be a published author to be seen as an industry expert—speaking engagements and the like are already taking care of that.

That said, consider these questions when thinking about making the decision to write your book...

5 Questions to Identify If You're Ready to Become a Published Author

1. How important is it to you? Unlike other business things we "have to do," becoming an author is purely optional. In fact, most of my clients see being published as first realizing a personal dream and second as a way to benefit their business. If you don't have a personal attachment to either of those reasons, this may not be the time for you to make the decision to write your book.

2. What is the upside of being an author? Identifying the benefits and keeping them front and center go along way to making a decision stick. Going back to my gym membership analogy, when we do start thinking about the benefits of going to the gym—being in better physical health, taking less medication, being able to buy clothes in a smaller size—the "grunt work" of actually lifting the weights or putting in the time on the elliptical is easier to do. If the benefits of being an author speak to your heart, you'll have an easier time making the time and committing to the resources that will see you through to publishing.

3. What's the downside of being an author? If you think "none," think again. It requires commitment—do you have it? And, these days, it doesn't end with the book. Most authors leapfrog to other info-products, such as audio CDs to accompany their books, or find themselves on the road more to speak about their book's topic. That can bring on a whole new set of decisions and actions you're not ready to take on right now. You have to be ready and willing for that kind of activity and, yes, success.

4. What don't you know? It's so empowering to identify what we don't know. Once we do that, it's easier to decide to turn to others who do know and have them take over that area. Like I always say, you're already busy in your business—you don't have time to become a publishing expert on top of everything else. The key is finding the resources and the people who do.

5. Are you willing to use resources other than yourself? One of both the positives and negatives of being an entrepreneur or business owner is that we get used to doing everything ourselves. That stick-to-it-ness serves us well when we're going the extra mile to serve a client, but it can also hold us back from achieving our dreams when we feel we have to complete every step of the process as a "lone wolf." Again, although I have full confidence in you and what you can achieve, there are some resources ad products that can take care of things much more efficiently and reasonably because it's their specific job to do so.

These are all items to consider before saying "I do. I really, really, really do" to your book project. But once you make that commitment, you'll find the road much, much smoother. There is power in making a decision.

■ ■ ■

This Mission, Should You Choose to Accept It...

In many ways, your book is like your business. And, like most successful businesses, it should have a mission statement.

We're so inundated with reading material that you have to give it your all to capture and keep a person's attention. The way you do that is give them a clear idea of what it is you will deliver in your book and what the reader will receive. And the way you do is by putting it in ink for everyone to see, including yourself.

Your book's mission statement is a few sentences that "tell all in a nutshell." If you have a clear idea of what your book is all about, it won't be that difficult to determine your mission statement. If you're finding it hard to describe the essence of your work, though, a good place to start is by answering the basic questions of journalism.

- Who: What is about you and your expertise that you're the one to write this book?
- What: Briefly mention the subjects you'll be covering
- Why: Describe why these subjects are important
- How: Describe how you will do this, for instance using true-life examples, stories or a step-by-step plan.

Wondering where the "where and when" are at? Actually, they are both givens—the "where" is in the book being held in hand and the "when" is now. Plus, here's a bonus tip for stronger writing: never start a sentence with the "when" element. It's usually the least important aspect of the information you're delivering.

Some additional qualities of your book's mission statement:
1. It's tied to your "end vision" of how you will use the book as your "big business card."

2. It says a great deal in a few words.

3. It's a "working paragraph." In other words, it may change as the book develops.

4. It will give you clarity about "what to include" and "what to leave out" as you write your book.

5. It identifies your reader, or who has the most to gain from reading your book.

Examples of authors and their books' mission statements:

Matt Heinz, author of *Move the Mouse & Make Millions*:
"This book is dedicated to helping small business managers and owners build and maintain a successful, profitable Web marketing strategy. Its focus is on giving you simple but effective steps to grow your business, win more clients and make more money by taking better advantage of the powerful consumer reach the Internet has to offer."

Rick Vassar, author of *Hide! Here Comes the Insurance Guy*:
"This is what the Insurance Guy series is all about: simple explanations, practical solutions and time-tested strategies that will reap huge savings in insurance costs...mapped out to be not just an initial learning tool but also an ongoing resource...the first section is an overview of business insurance....the second section explains the most basic insurance coverage...the third section is the glossary..."

Peter Wallin, author of *In Pursuit of Business:*
> "I am addressing business owners who seriously want to grow their business...I will take over two decades of experience and give it all to you in an easy-to-digest manner. I will share my success stories and, yes, my failures. Through it all you will see how I fit the importance of proper thinking, planning and building relationships into my game plan."

Sally Stewart, author of *Media Training 101:*
> "*Media Training 101* is an in-depth guide to handling the news media written by a seasoned journalist and public relations professional. A former *USA Today* reporter and consultant to major companies, Sally Stewart leads you through every step in developing a communications blueprint and a strategic public relations plan to support it."

Mission statements come in all shapes and sizes, first person and third. Notice, though, how these mission statements tightly explain the essence of what's to come. That's the key and the first step into getting your book on track to being a successful "big business card."

In addition, besides keeping you on track when you're writing your masterpiece, your mission statement is the start of your marketing message appearing on book jackets, Amazon listings and other places needing a quick and strong description of your book.

Keep writing and rewriting your mission statement until it is crisp, clean and powerful! It will make the rest of your book writing process super easy. (And we like easy!)

■ ■ ■

When You Have Too Much Content…Or Not Enough

If you're like many aspiring authors, one of the questions you're most likely asking is: "What should my book be about?"

In fact, it may be that very question that's been holding you back in getting your book done. After all, you don't want to spend hours and hours of your time to "write the wrong book" and find it's not of interest to anyone. Trust me, it's embarrassing to write a book no one wants to read—I know because I did it myself!

Below are two of my tried-and-true solutions for selecting a winning book subject.

The first problem many people face is having too much material and balk at the thought of wading through loads of articles, blog posts, transcriptions and more. It can be overwhelming to even think about picking "just one thing" to concentrate on for your book.

If "information overload" is your problem, what I recommend is to first think about your core message. What is the overriding theme of your work? What "one thing" do you know above all else—a belief or a part of a system that differentiates you from others in your field? Once you identify that one message and can describe it in 3-5 sentences, flag the information related to just that subject and build your book's content around it.

Another solution is to narrow your focus by making your book a "case study" of one of your greatest success stories. Why is this effective? Because it essentially tells a good story, which is always interesting to readers, and then showcases your expertise as you solved the problems the case study subject presented—essentially making YOU THE HERO!

Another common problem is not having ANY written material to start with. Perhaps you're new to your business or have been forced to make a transition from the traditional workforce and strike out on your own.

If you are just getting started in your field, you can apply the same "case study and succeed story" technique as above, even if you have ZERO clients (yet perhaps friend who could use your help and is willing to be a "guinea pig."). Take good notes along the way and not only will you have everything you need for your book, you'll be putting in place sound business practices for future clients.

Or, if you find yourself new to your field, or branching off into a different area, you are in the beautiful position of starting with a clean slate and have the ability to define yourself the way YOU want to be perceived among your target audience.

Since you probably want to be perceived as a problem-solver, survey (electronically or in person) the members of your target audience on what it is they want to know about your area of expertise, and then answer the questions and present your solutions in your book.

By the way, don't worry about "giving it all away." Give your best stuff in your book—it will establish you as an expert and you'll be sought after by people wanting more.

■ ■ ■

How to Write Your Book Fast

When I wanted to increase my weight loss results, my trainer encouraged me to do intervals. So now I pepper my hour-long walks with 3 or 4 times when I flat out run. (Think Phoebe from "Friends," but not quite as graceful.)

The interval training accomplishes things for me on several fronts: it gets my heart racing in the moment as I'm physically pushing myself to move with more speed, plus it gets me to my end goal faster (literally & figuratively).

After I was done with my last session, the small part of my brain not busy taking in as much oxygen as possible came up with a connection between interval training and book writing: in both cases, short bursts of speed work means you can get your book done a lot faster than you ever thought possible.

It's exactly how you can write a book. Here is how you can apply "intervals" to your schedule to make big progress on your book or, actually, any project you find hanging over your head:

1. Concentrated effort. Make a quick list of what you have to do to get your book done. Break down the items so that each one, with dedicated effort, will take between 20 minutes and an hour.

   These items might range from doing some market research to creating a table of contents or outlining a chapter. Then peg which one of those items is the next step to getting your book done. Commit to working on that item—and only that item—for the next period of time you designate as "book writing time."

2. No distractions. Shut down your Internet browser and, yes, your email. (Although it pains me to say it, I have to admit that it's probably one of the biggest time sucks around.) Shut the door. Unplug your phone—that's why there's voicemail.

3. Work in short bursts. There's a reason we can't work so intensely all the time: it's effective, but draining. So set the clock and work in shorter periods of time—50 minutes is ideal, but you'll still get a lot done if it's only 20 or 30 minutes. The key is to focus 100 percent of your energy to getting this next step done, done, done.

4. Make your last push the strongest. My fitness trainer says the last interval is the most important. That's when she recommends pushing yourself so that at the end you're absolutely spent—but kind of impressed with yourself and what you accomplished. The same with your book writing interval time. You might be tempted to stop with a few minutes left, but I encourage you to push yourself to follow through on your commitment and get that final burst of thought out of your head and onto the screen or page. It can be that extra effort that causes the whole project to take a big leap forward.

5. Celebrate! I usually end my interval training mornings with a half-decaf-sugar-free-vanilla non-fat latte, but sometimes I choose to take an extra spin around the block (in my car) while singing along real loud with a favorite song (not "Smelly Cat"). It doesn't matter how you decide to pat yourself on the back—just be sure to do it. Trust me, it will make that next writing "workout" that much easier.

There you have it! My step-by-step methodology I use to show others how to write a book. You know what works for you, too, so take some of these ideas, meld them with your own and, this is key, get started RIGHT NOW!

Send me an autographed copy of your book and I'll give you a special gift—plus know your book will go in the "Shelf of Fame" stationed in my office. For my current mailing address, email Info@MyBigBusinessCard.com

■ ■ ■

Insider Strategy
#7

The Case Study Book

Want to write a book to serve as a "big business card" but cringing at the thought of tooting your own horn? It's the "case study book" to the rescue!

A content of the book centers on telling the success stories of your clients. As you do, the reader will see great examples of your expertise and professionalism "at work." Other benefits of the case study book include providing a formula meaning your book is easy to write, plus people love reading stories. Case studies are, in essence, compelling stories that will keep your reader engaged from beginning to end—showcasing your expertise and building your credibility with every word.

Here are the basic steps for creating a case study book.

1. Identify your subjects. I recommend 5–10 per book, depending on how long your stories will be.

Important note: The reader will instantly recognize themselves in your studies and will contact you to find out how you can help them, so make sure you write about clients you enjoyed working with and want to attract more of!

2. Follow this formula for each case study:
   ▶ Give the client's background and situation
   ▶ Identify the challenges the client presented
   ▶ Describe what your solution was to those challenges
   ▶ Detail the results your client had from following your input

Important note: Be sure to each section is fleshed out thoroughly, especially the challenges the client presented. You want to describe their problems fully so the reader realizes the power of the end results.

3. Many "Write a Book in a Weekend" participants ask me if they should get permission or change names or create composites for their case studies. Although it depends on the situation, I recommend, if possible, to use "real case scenarios" that include real names and situations—that gives your case study added credibility. If your work is of a more sensitive nature, however, using different names and situations or creating a composite of clients in one case study is perfectly okay. The point is to create a compelling story that will engage the reader while exhibiting what you can do for them, too.

In this section I provide some "light" case studies taken from my monthly "hard copy" newsletter. In a future book I plan to expand them to show the challenges each of these authors overcame to write their first book.

Case Study: **Meredith Liepelt**

Her Book: *Flourish! Ten Easy, Elegant and Essential Marketing Strategies for Solo- and Micropreneurs*

Donna Notes: *During the "Write a Book in a Weekend," Meredith set a clear intention kept focus, successfully putting together more than 15,000 words for her book by Sunday night. I was so impressed, I brought her back to speak to a later "class," where she provided great encouragement and how-to-do-it expertise.*

Meredith is from Dublin, Ohio, and is president of www.RichLifeMarketing.com. She's a coach, speaker, and award-winning client attraction strategist. She is a featured columnist in Glow Magazine and has been seen and heard on television and radio shows around the country.

I caught up with Meredith to see how things have progressed since her book was published.

Donna: Meredith, describe "what is that you do."

Meredith: I teach women solopreneurs how to creatively raise their profile, attract ideal clients and develop a variety of simple income streams to increase their income.

D: Now that your book's done what's next for you in your business?

M: I'm creating new private and group coaching programs. I understand that people are tired of traditional expensive group coaching programs with little one-on-one time with the coach. I'm developing a new creative way to meet the needs of my clients as well as my own. I'm very excited about this!

D: What was the biggest hurdle you got over on the road to writing your book?

M: I have several books in my head that I want to write and I had a hard time knowing which one to select. I ended up realizing that any one of them would serve as my "big business card," as Donna calls it, and would open doors for me, which is exactly what has happened. My intention was to have a book with fantastic content and a super-cool cover. And now I have it!

D: Do you have a favorite quote?

M: "The difference between 'try' and 'triumph,' is just a little 'umph.'"~ Bonnie Przybylski

D: What's the best lesson you've taken away from writing your book?

M: What seems impossible actually *is* possible when you fully commit to it and get the support you need.

To find out more about Meredith, take advantage of her services or obtain a copy of her book, you can catch up to her at www.Twitter.com/MeredithLiepelt or www.Facebook.com/MeredithLiepelt or visit her website at www.RichLifeMarketing.com.

Case Study:	Vicki Ehlers
Her Book:	*Green at Birth: Smart Moms Create Nature Connections for Infants and Toddlers*

Donna Notes: *Vicki holds a special place in my heart because she is the first "Write a Book in a Weekend" graduate who completed her book and sent me a copy. The day it arrived, I sat on my sofa with a cup of tea and read every word of it. Vicki and I have remained close and did some work together to create her online presence too. Vicki Ehlers, of Stillwater, Oklahoma, is a mom, consultant, educator and coach. She has combined her love of children, education and nature to do her part to help everyone "embrace their green side."*

I asked Vicki how things are going since she finished writing her book.

Donna: Vicki, describe what is that you do.

Vicki: I support parents and educators in developing relationships and environments to nurture very young children. As an educator, consultant, and coach, I help others discover how play, nurturing relationships, and connections to nature can bring a sense of well-being to young children and their grown-ups. I give people of all ages an invitation to celebrate the wonders of play-filled childhoods!

D: Now that your book's done what's next for you in your business?

V: My little book is the springboard for creating on online business. I am having fun learning how to share my passion, resources, and experience through online connections. My book is also serving as an expanded business card for the work I do as an educator in my local community.

D: What was the biggest hurdle you got over on the road to writing your book?

V: The biggest ah-ha! was discovering that my book didn't have to be a thick, scholarly textbook that took ages to write. It's a worthwhile endeavor to create a small book on a single topic as a way to share your passion and purpose with others.

D: Do you have a favorite quote?

V: "Wisdom begins with wonder." ~ Socrates

D: What's the next big thing on your goal list?

V: To develop an online group coaching program on creating nature connections for moms of toddlers.

D: What's the best lesson you've taken away from writing your book?

V: There are many people who want to connect with you and your work through the written word. Create your book and have fun sharing it!

If you would like to know more about Vicki, take advantage of her services or obtain a copy of her book, you can catch up to her at www.twitter.com/VickiEhlers or www.facebook.com/VickiEhlers or visit her website at www.greenatbirth.com.

Case Study:	Ron West
His Book:	*The Perfect Life – A Personal Journey of Relationship Healing*

Donna Notes: *Ron was one of my "Write a Book in a Weekend" participants to write a book that had nothing to do with his business or creating a big business card for himself. His book is a legacy left to his family centered around passing on the benefits of what he has learned about relationships to his children and grandchildren. Now that he has expressed that message, he's proceeding with a number of other books to support his growing coaching business and workshops. From Indianapolis, Indiana, Ron is a coach, consultant, facilitator, speaker and writer whose focus is on transforming businesses.*

I checked in with Ron to see how things have been going since he finished his book and here is some of what he had to say.

Donna: **Ron, how do you help businesses to transform?**

Ron: Companies cross geographic, cultural, political, and religious boundaries. I help business leaders shift the way they are BEing to bring about a fundamental change in the way they DO business. I'm kind of a corporate shaman.

D: What was the purpose behind writing a book that didn't have anything to do with your business?

R: This first book was only ever intended for my family. I was hoping to ensure that some of the things I learned about relationships might benefit my children or perhaps their children. While my manuscript was being proofread someone in the office read the whole thing and left inspired enough to write their own story. Is it not wonderful how ripples in a pond work? You never know the impact your message may have on another. I have decided to write a sequel for men—a book that helps guide them through a process of personal healing and reconciliation.

D: What was the biggest hurdle you got over on the road to writing your book?

R: MYSELF. It is really interesting how any challenge brings up the same limiting beliefs that have held us back in every endeavor. There is much wisdom in the phrase "just do it!" The first book served two purposes. I wanted to overcome a limiting belief that I had about not knowing enough and needing all the answers before I could start writing. Sound familiar? The second was to release some of my other limiting beliefs so I could move on with my life and BE all I dreamed I could BE.

D: What's the next "big" thing on your goal list?

R: I have already taken part in another *Write a Book in a Weekend* event and made huge progress on my second book. It is an eBook and the first in a series of ten that addresses how a whole organization can recognize and shift out of a victim mindset to a level of conscious responsibility.

D: As a graduate of our program and a newly published author, what's the best lesson you've taken away from the experience?

R: It is way easier once you get started. The fear melts away.

D: Sum it all up with a quote, Ron.

R: "Man needs for his happiness, not only the enjoyment of this or that, but hope and enterprise and change." ~Bertrand Russell

If you would like to get in touch with Ron you can reach him at ron@jwest.com or look him up at LinkedIn.

Case Study: Sandy Goodwin

Her Book: *I Think, Therefore I Doubt: 12 Key Principles to Build Self-Confidence & Self-Trust: For Perfectionists, People-Pleasers, & Heart-Centered Women*

Donna Notes: *Another one of my favorites, Sandy Goodwin is an "Inner Confidence Coach" who shares her wisdom about overcoming perfectionism—one of my favorite audio interviews is one we did where she gave "Write a Book in a Weekend" participants tips about putting aside their "Inner Critic" so they can get their book done. She and I also created a created a virtual book tour audio, the first product connected with her book.*

Sandy, of Monterey Bay, California, first got the coaching bug as an operating room nurse in the United States Air Force where she began helping patients to move through their fears. Later, as a nursing instructor, she started coaching her students to take small steps to build their inner confidence. Sandy has been coaching college students and educators for over 20 years and is a Certified Fearless Living Coach as well as a Mentor in the Fearless Living™ Institute Coaching Program.

Sandy took the time to fill me in about what she has been up to since completing her book.

Donna: Sandy, tell us a little bit about what you do.

Sandy: I'm an Inner Confidence Coach for women. I help women trust and believe in themselves so they can stop doubting and start doing whatever their heart desires.

D: Now that your book's done how are you using it for your business?

S: I have a book preview webpage and my book is now listed on the products page of my website, and I am promoting those through my e-newsletter, Twitter, and Facebook. I am also working on creating teleseminars and a group program to go more indepth and interactive with the content in my book.

D: What was the biggest hurdle you got over on the road to writing your book?

S: My biggest hurdle was trying to sift through all the possibilities and information out there about writing a book. I wanted a simple step-by-step approach (like what I do for my clients to help them move forward). Your *Write a Book in a Weekend Program* supported me with that process. I had specific book writing tasks to do one step at a time, with guidance, so I could move forward and keep going.

D: Do you have a favorite quote?

S: My personal mantra is: "Stop waiting for the perfect and start doing the good enough." One of my favorite quotes from my book is "It's not who you are that holds you back, it's who you think you're not." ~ Unknown Author

D: As a graduate of our program and a newly published author, what's the best lesson you've taken away from the experience?

S: The best lesson is that it's possible! Anything is possible if you decide you really want to do it and keep going even when you want to stop.

If you would like to know more about Sandy or her Coaching Services you can catch up to her at www.Twitter.com/CoachSandyG, www.Facebook.com/SandyGoodwin, or you can visit her website at www.innerconfidencecoach.com. For a free preview of Sandy's book go to www.IThinkThereforeIDoubt.com.

Bringing It All Together

> "It is not enough to be busy…the question is:
> What are we busy about?"
>
> ~ Henry David Thoreau

I still have moments of "how did I get here" when I hear people introduce me at events and on teleseminars. It's true that I grew up on a 200-acre dairy farm in northwestern Pennsylvania—I really loved the life of fresh air and creativity brought on by having to make up my entertainment when told "go out and play" under the big tree in the front yard.

On one of those days, when I was about seven years old, I wrote my first book. It was several sheets of lined tablet paper folded over and trimmed into "book size." The title: "The Autobiography of Donna Kozik" by Donna Kozik. Yes, it was a short book, but it had words and illustrations and even a Swingline stapler binding. My Mom thought it was the greatest thing she ever read and that day I became a writer for a lifetime.

I was surprised as anybody at the success brought on by my first book, *29 Days to a Smooth Move.* Still a strong seller in the home "do it yourself" section of Amazon, getting mentions in all the magazines and newspapers wasn't that difficult—in fact, the hardest thing was getting the book written. As I worked with other clients to get theirs done, it wasn't long before my mind was searching for a faster and easier way for people to publish their "big business card" and accomplish a life-long dream.

If you are a coach, consultant or entrepreneur you know the benefits of being a published author. A book establishes your expertise, builds your credibility and can be used in a number of ways to generate more warm leads, hot prospects and steady clients. Plus, the additional exposure your book brings you means you can raise your fees and people will pay it—no questions asked! In fact, you probably realize that **having your book has become as necessary as having a website or a business card**—in fact, your book *is* your business card.

A book has become a proven way to attract more engagements, generate back-of-room sales and provide a starting point for other info products.

So I brought it all together with this book, based on what I've discovered and taught from my virtual "Write a Book in a Weekend" events, featuring my "fill-in-the-blanks" book template plus a weekend of live audio and recorded video messages that motivate and inspire soon-to-be authors to complete their books in two days.

Here is a recap of my insider strategies:

1. Get Cooking on Your Book & Recite Your Favorite Recipe

There is something you do well and effortlessly. Pinpoint what that is and build your book on describing, down to the nitty gritty, how you do it.

2. Write Your Book Like You Would Clean Your Closet

If you get overwhelmed at the thought of how to organize all your material in a book, think of your ideas as outfits and include only the most dazzling ones.

3. Visualize Your Book & Download It into Reality

Make your book real by creating a prototype complete with title, testimonials and your picture on the cover.

4. Self-Publish or Traditional Publish?

Technology means that no one can tell the difference—the point is to get your book in print.

When it comes to the type of book you can write in a weekend, I recommend the "short and powerful" book and showcase these examples with mini-books included in this publication:

 # 5 **"The Quote Book"**

Collect your favorite quotations and put them in a book. If you like to add some "oomph," write what the quote means to you and give the reader an action step.

 # 6 **"The Case Study Book"**

Highlight your work by telling stories of clients who have succeeded using your methods.

 # 7 **"The Ezine Article/Blog Posting Book"**

Recycle your material—and re-emphasize your messages—by putting previously written pieces in a book. Add a little bit here, polish a little bit there, and you're done!

With this book, I've looked to give you at least one idea of a book you could write—maybe in as little as a weekend. In any case, no matter how you choose to write your book and become a published author, I wish you the absolute best of success!

Words of Appreciation & Resources

"My Testimonial is a Really Big Thank You!"

"I just want to say that I absolutely loved the process. I wasn't a doubter if I could do it or not. I just have a really hard time focusing, and I was just thrilled with what happened to me.

"It's been a really long time since I've been involved in something where I didn't want to stop doing it. Whenever I stood up and stretched, I couldn't wait to get back to it. Only had that experience when working on an art project—I was so immersed in it.

"The whole workshop was put together to help to give a focus for to crank out something that I already had in me. My testimonial is a really big 'thank you' for the heartfelt focus you had to help me do this.

Susannah Weiss
Washington DC
SuzWorks.org

"You Gave Me Specific Action Steps for a Head Start"

"I've watched how you've helped other entrepreneurs, professionals and coaches become recognized experts in their field by having a book to hand out as a 'big business card.'

"I love the concept—what's been holding me back is how do I write that book? And the 'Write a Book in a Weekend' event says I can do it now.

"Also, I'm very thankful for you. As soon as I registered you gave me some wonderful advice to get a head start and take my energy and channel it into some very specific actions to give me a head start on my book and use that book to build my business.

"Thank you for going that extra mile!"

Joe Paul
Dallas-Ft. Worth, Texas
Leadership Management Institute

"You Had the Experience & Knowledge to Pull It All Together"

"I wanted to thank you for giving myself permission to take a weekend for myself and work on a book I've been wanting to write for awhile.

"I haven't written anything for myself for a long time…I've been wanting to move more from offering my services into creating info-products.

"You really had the experience and the knowledge to pull it all together. The calls, email, templates and tools were supportive to allow us to walk in there and get it done.

"I would highly recommend this to anyone who says "you know, someday I want to write a book…"

Andrea Glass
San Diego, Calif.

"I Completed Two Books...and Came Up with a Whole Platform of Products!"

"I was absolutely blown away by the 'Write a Book in a Weekend' online event.

"I'm a serial entrepreneur and have all these great ideas I've started, but not finished. Ideas, half finished books…those can't be sold, can't be given away and do absolutely nothing for your business.

"At the end of the weekend, not only had I completed one book, but two. And I had come up with a whole platform of products…completed products and completed books that can be given away and sold.

"One of the best parts of this weekend was the defined structure—and it was very easy to do!"

David Di Francesco
Long Beach, CA
WarriorWorkout.com

"Donna Makes It Easy!"

"I love working with Donna because she makes it easy. I have so much going on and just feel overwhelmed with everything I should be doing, but Donna has a special way of simplifying complex things.

"I tend to be a perfectionist and often hesitate not knowing what to write or say. But, Donna's easy-going nature and encouragement gets my creativity flowing. Her simple templates are great at getting my ideas from my head to paper to a finished product.

"Plus, she is fun! Life is short and if you're going to be running your own business, you might as well work with people you enjoy. Thanks for being such a positive, encouraging energy that keeps me going."

~ Jeanie Callen Barat, "The Fitness Jeanie"
San Diego, Calif.

Get Your Free Companion Audio & Resource Guide Here

"Inside Author Tips: 5 Sizzling Strategies to Get Your Book Done on the Double"

Featuring two-time award winning author Donna Kozik (as seen in *Woman's Day* & *Women's World* magazines, plus heard on NPR's "Marketplace")

Listen to this companion audio and discover:

1. The single most important reason why most people never get their book done. (Never fall prey to it again!)
2. 5 simple strategies that will allow you to get your book done in your "spare time".
3. Insider secrets to writing the kind of book that everyone wants to read! Get the scoop on what turns a "blah" book into a "best seller" material.
4. 3 proven methods to "write without writing" for writingphobes and those who fear writer's block!
5. Mindset mastery. How to stop procrastinating and "getting in your own way" when it comes to writing or finishing your book. Donna notes: This might be listed last but I've found that it's the most important item that turns "wannabe" writers into published authors.

You're guaranteed to be inspired and ready to get started writing your own masterpiece or "big business card."

Get your FREE companion audio at
www.MyBigBusinessCard.com/fivestrategies

"Give me the straight scoop. What's this 'Write a Book in a Weekend' all about?"

It's a "virtual" online weekend, when you can create the one item that can lead you to:

- Get more of the highly coveted clients you desire
- Charge higher fees—even as much as quadrupling your current asking price
- Establish your expertise overnight—expertise that you don't have to explain because no one will question you
- Speak volumes about your professional knowledge and credibility—24 hours a day, 7 days a week!

There's a way to achieve those items and much more—including a feeling of self-satisfaction in doing something so many just dream of doing...

Becoming a published author.

In fact, you probably realize that having your book has become as necessary as having a website or a business card—your book is your business card.

A book has become a proven way to attract more engagements, generate back-of-room sales and provide a starting point for other info products.

Other benefits of having a book include:

- Establishing credibility and expertise in your field
- "Speaks" for you 24/7

- ▶ Serves as a lead generator and client attraction tool
- ▶ Thanks to technology, easier to publish—for only a few dollars—than ever before

The problem is...you still have to write it!

What generally gets in the way of doing that is:

- ▶ Finding the time
- ▶ Determining what to write about, whether you're narrowing down a broad topic or "starting from scratch"
- ▶ Figuring out how to organize your materials
- ▶ Banishing your inner critic
- ▶ Knowing if you're on the right path

Before I go on, I want to give you a few starter solutions:

1. Write a "short and powerful" book— that is short on content, but still powerful in message (and can be written fast!)

2. Types of short and powerful books you can write include a quote book, a book of case studies, even a book based on questions you receive all the time. (If people are asking, they want to know.)

3. Still stuck? Look to your email "sent" box for material you've already written. Some of the answers you email in response to client questions can practically be taken word for word and put in a book.

This gives you a clearer direction and can make it seem more manageable.

Umm, of course, you STILL have to write it!

Words of Appreciation and Resources

That's why I developed the "Write a Book in a Weekend" virtual event. It's a program and a system to literally have you write a book in a weekend. (Plus give you the publishing know-how so you can have a copy in hand the following week!)

I'll tell you in a moment how you can register…plus get a free gift from me.

But first, here are some highlights of my "Write a Book in a Weekend" system:

- ▶ Write from the comfort of your own home (no travel necessary)
- ▶ Still get the "event" feel with people you can network with
- ▶ Book "templates" take care of the formatting for you
- ▶ An expert "book writing coach" giving you feedback and answering your questions
- ▶ An "after care" program that shows you what to do after the weekend to market yourself and your book
- ▶ Bonus audios about selecting a winning title, organizing your material, effectively scheduling your time and much, much more.

To find when the next "Write a Book in a Weekend" Event is, visit www.WriteWithDonna.com. While you're there, register for my free audio, "12 Strategies to Publishing Success," plus pick up your copy of my free publishing resource guide.